MRJC

TULSA CITY COUNTY LIBRARY

D1528645

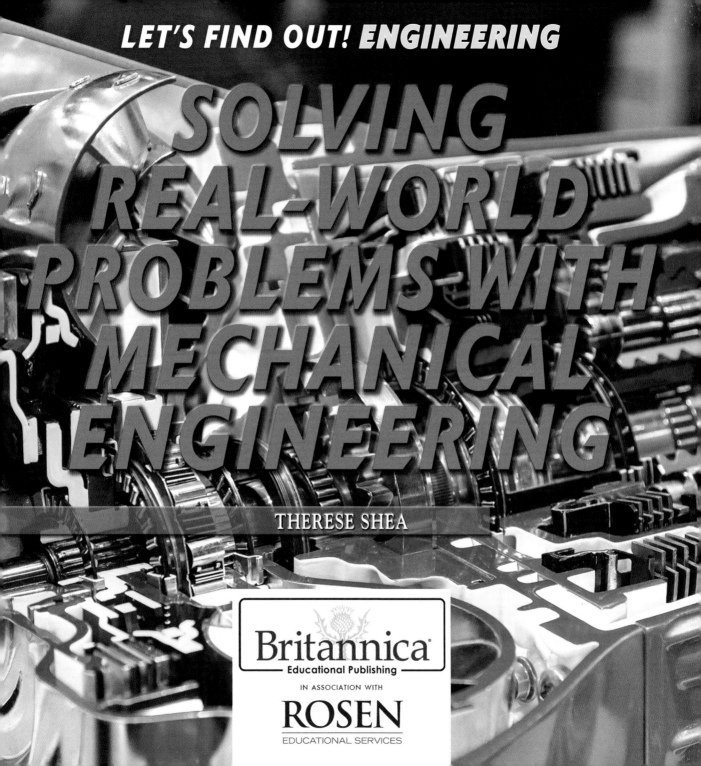

LET'S FIND OUT! ENGINEERING

SOLVING REAL-WORLD PROBLEMS WITH MECHANICAL ENGINEERING

THERESE SHEA

Britannica®
Educational Publishing

IN ASSOCIATION WITH

ROSEN
EDUCATIONAL SERVICES

Published in 2016 by Britannica Educational Publishing (a trademark of Encyclopædia Britannica, Inc.) in association with The Rosen Publishing Group, Inc.
29 East 21st Street, New York, NY 10010

Copyright © 2016 The Rosen Publishing Group, Inc., and Encyclopædia Britannica, Inc. Encyclopaedia Britannica, Britannica, and the Thistle logo are registered trademarks of Encyclopædia Britannica, Inc. All rights reserved.

Distributed exclusively by Rosen Publishing.
To see additional Britannica Educational Publishing titles, go to rosenpublishing.com.

First Edition

Britannica Educational Publishing
J.E. Luebering: Director, Core Reference Group
Mary Rose McCudden: Editor, Britannica Student Encyclopedia

Rosen Publishing
Shalini Saxena: Editor
Nelson Sá: Art Director
Nicole Russo: Designer
Cindy Reiman: Photography Manager
Carina Finn: Photo Researcher

Library of Congress Cataloging-in-Publication Data

Shea, Therese, author.
 Solving real-world problems with mechanical engineering / [Author] Therese Shea. — First edition.
   pages cm. — (Let's find out! Engineering)
 Includes bibliographical references and index.
 ISBN 978-1-68048-266-9 (library bound) — ISBN 978-1-5081-0079-9 (pbk.) — ISBN 978-1-68048-323-9 (6-pack)
 1. Mechanical engineering—Juvenile literature. 2. Mechanical engineers—Juvenile literature. I. Title.

 TJ147.S54 2016
 621—dc23

                                                                                              2015016640

Manufactured in the United States of America

Photo credits: Cover, p. 1, interior pages background image Anna Vaczi/Shutterstock.com; pp. 4, 7, 11, 21 Encyclopædia Britannica, Inc.; p. 5 Northfoto/Shutterstock.com; p. 6 Digital Vision/Photodisc/Thinkstock; p. 8 British Crown copyright, Science Museum, London; p. 9 Heritage Images/Hulton Archive/Getty Images; p. 10 © iStockphoto.com/ paule858; p. 12 Library of Congress, Washington, D.C. (digital no. 3b11564); p. 13 Stockbyte/Thinkstock; p. 14 Library of Congress, Washington, D.C.; pp. 15, 16 Universal History Archive/Universal Images Group/Getty Images; pp. 17, 27 Echo/Cultura/Getty Images; p. 18 FPG/Hulton Archive/Getty Images; p. 19 Art-Of-Photo/iStock/Thinkstock; p. 20 ullstein bild/Getty Images; p. 22 Roger Dale Pleis/Shutterstock.com; p. 23 Michelle Del Guercio/Science Source/Getty Images; p. 24 Yoshikazu Tsuno/AFP/Getty Images; p. 25 Spencer Platt/Getty Images; p. 26 Tyler Olson/Shutterstock. com; p. 28 artjazz/Shutterstock.com; p. 29 Ariel Skelly/Blend Images/Getty Images

CONTENTS

Engineers in the Real World

Engineers are people who use science and math to solve problems with products, structures, or processes. Sometimes they help develop new products, structures, or processes. They also fix and improve existing ones.

There are several kinds of engineering. The main kinds are civil, chemical, electrical, and mechanical engineering. Civil engineers focus on the building of structures, such as bridges. Chemical engineers develop

Machines can be simple, like the ones here, or more complicated.

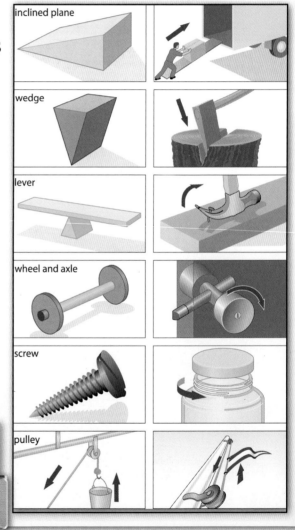

inclined plane

wedge

lever

wheel and axle

screw

pulley

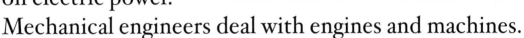

Aerospace engineers work on a device that will be used on a spacecraft.

chemicals for businesses. Electrical engineers focus on electric power. Mechanical engineers deal with engines and machines.

Each of these four branches can be broken down into even more specialized types of engineering. For example, some electrical engineers focus on computers. Some mechanical engineers work on developing and improving aircraft and spacecraft. They are called aerospace engineers.

Think About It

Besides creating machines and building structures, engineers may develop better methods, or ways, of doing things. Think of a time you followed steps to make something and discovered a better way to do it.

Machines, Motion, and More

Mechanical engineering deals with everything surrounding machines. This includes designing, making, and operating them, as well as setting them up. Mechanical engineering can mean anything from constructing a car engine to overseeing a power plant.

Mechanical engineers are also concerned with motion and the forces that affect motion. A force is anything that acts on the position of an object. A force may put an object into motion, or it can have an effect on the speed of that motion. Basically, force means a push or pull. Friction is one kind of

These engineers help take care of machines that provide energy in a nuclear power station.

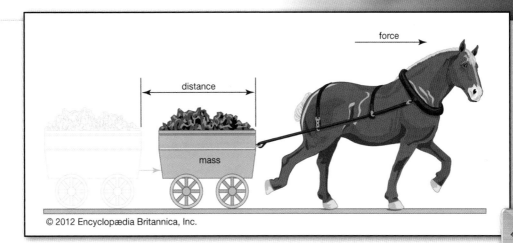

force

distance

mass

© 2012 Encyclopædia Britannica, Inc.

force mechanical engineers have to think about. This force stops movement between two surfaces that touch.

As this drawing shows, the force of the horse's pull puts the cart into motion.

Mechanical engineers follow a process when trying to solve a problem. They research as much as they can about it. Then they design a possible solution and develop it. Next, they test the solution and perfect it. They may redesign the solution if it does not solve the problem.

COMPARE AND CONTRAST

Mechanical engineers often have to deal with the force of friction. How is this different from a force like gravity? How might these forces affect an object?

Start with the Steam Engine

The development of the steam engine at the end of the 18th century is an example of mechanical engineers improving a product that already existed. The first steam engine was actually invented in the 1st century!

Energy makes things move. Machines need energy to work. The improved steam engine used the pressure of hot steam as an energy source to move parts within it. The movement of these parts, in turn, could turn a wheel or do some other kind of

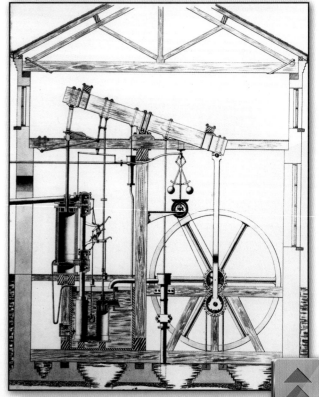

Inventor James Watt designed this steam engine. The drawing dates from 1788.

work. Later, this work was producing electric power.

The steam engine helped spread the use of machines in certain parts of the world for the first time. This launched the Industrial Revolution. It also led to the founding of mechanical engineering as a new, separate branch of engineering.

The **Industrial Revolution** began in the 18th century, when people began using machines in factories to make products rather than making the products by hand. This meant many more products could be made in a shorter period of time.

This drawing shows a workshop in England where steam engines were built.

9

POWER PRODUCERS

The steam engine provided an effective way of producing power from heat. Before this, power sources included wind, water, and muscle—both animal and human. One of the first challenges of early mechanical engineers was to increase power.

They did this by developing a steam turbine powered by large steam boilers. A steam turbine is more powerful than a steam engine. A turbine is an engine with a part made up of blades. In a steam turbine, steam from a boiler causes

Turbine generators in a hydroelectric power plant help turn the power of water into electricity.

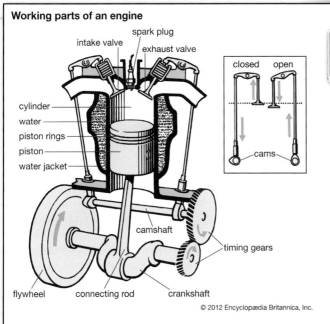

Working parts of an engine

intake valve
spark plug
exhaust valve

closed   open

cylinder
water
piston rings
piston
water jacket

cams

camshaft

timing gears

flywheel   connecting rod   crankshaft

© 2012 Encyclopædia Britannica, Inc.

Internal combustion engines, like this one, can be found in different vehicles.

the blades to rotate, which creates power. Today, powerful turbines drive electric generators in power plants, providing energy for communities.

Mechanical engineers also developed internal combustion engines. They discovered that a fuel, such as gasoline or diesel, can be burned in air to create a hot, expanding gas. The resulting force can power an engine's parts. Internal combustion engines are used in cars, trucks, ships, trains, and aircraft.

Combustion is a chemical reaction that produces heat and light. Fire is the most common form.

Mass Production

Mechanical engineers developed—and are still developing—machines to produce goods. They even build the machines that build machines! Their work changed business. Products could be made faster and at a lower cost than if they were made by hand. Making products this way in such large numbers is called mass production. With machinery, products also had fewer mistakes and a steady level of quality.

For example, the mechanical assembly line completely

Completed Model T cars come off the Ford Motor Company assembly line in about 1917.

Assembly lines in factories today are more advanced than they were in 1917.

changed the automobile industry. Each worker on an assembly line does just one task on a product before passing it on to another worker to do another task on it and so on. Henry Ford designed several assembly lines in his automobile plant, perfecting the process. In 1913 the time it took to assemble one car went from over 12 hours to less than 3 hours! A greater number of cars were produced at lower cost, which meant more people could afford a car for the first time.

THINK ABOUT IT

Engineers who focus on producing goods think about speed, cost, and quality. Are there goods that cannot be made by machinery? Why?

Transportation Advances

From ancient times until the early 1800s, the only way to move loads over land was by using the strength of people and animals. Goods were usually pulled by one or more animals in a vehicle such as a wagon. Trips were often slow and sometimes dangerous.

Engineer Richard Trevithick created the first steam-powered locomotive in 1803. A locomotive is an engine that can power its own motion. Trevithick's locomotive had the pulling power of many horses and was used to

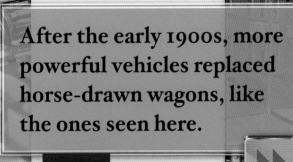

After the early 1900s, more powerful vehicles replaced horse-drawn wagons, like the ones seen here.

haul, or transport, coal. Soon, steam locomotives were hauling long lines of linked train cars full of passengers. Railroads helped to open up the central and western United States to both travelers and settlers. Later, electricity and then diesel fuel were used to power the engines of locomotives.

Richard Trevithick's locomotive amazed the public. Here, it is being shown to a crowd in 1809.

COMPARE AND CONTRAST

Railroads are still used to carry passengers and goods today, even though airplanes are faster. Why do you think this is?

The Wright brothers test a glider just two years before their famous flight.

Railroads made travel to faraway places easier. Yet, people wanted to go even farther, especially over oceans and mountains. It dawned on some engineers that flying was one way to cross these distances. Self-taught engineers Orville and Wilbur Wright designed, built, and flew the first airplane in 1903. Their first flight was just 12 seconds long, but it was a beginning.

Jet-powered aircraft were introduced during World War II (1939–1945). A jet engine moves a plane forward by shooting exhaust, or gases that escape from an

Engineers make sure all parts of an airplane are working before and after most flights.

engine, out the back. Today, passenger jets fly people around the world every day.

The mechanical engineers who built the earliest airplanes became specialized in learning about aerodynamics, the study of forces on objects moving through air. Aerospace engineering was born from that. Aerospace engineers and mechanical engineers may work together, especially when designing, or planning how to build, an aircraft.

THINK ABOUT IT

Aerospace engineers often start their studies with a mechanical engineering degree. Why do you think this is?

KEEPING IT COOL

Another impact that mechanical engineers have made on the world is the invention of refrigeration, which is the cooling of substances or spaces to low temperatures. The first mechanical refrigeration systems were developed in the mid-1800s but were used mostly for businesses. Some used huge motors and ammonia gas, which is poisonous. Refrigerators for homes—using safer chemicals and smaller motors—finally began to replace iceboxes

By the 1940s, refrigerators like this one made keeping food safe and fresh much easier than before.

In many ways, air conditioning has changed how people live. It makes being indoors on a hot summer day comfortable.

in the 1930s. Refrigeration made it possible to keep both food and medicine from spoiling for much longer than when they were kept in natural temperatures.

Air conditioning was a development that came from refrigeration systems. Air conditioning is the use of mechanical systems to control air quality in a space. Air conditioners usually make air cooler. They can also heat, circulate, clean, and add or reduce moisture in the air.

THINK ABOUT IT

Refrigeration meant perishable goods, such as certain kinds of food, could be transported long distances for the first time. Why was this important?

19

ENERGY FOR TODAY AND TOMORROW

Mechanical engineering has produced many useful products. However, many of these products have a negative effect on the environment. For example, gas-powered engines and coal-burning power plants cause water and air pollution. Such products require the use of fossil fuels, which are nonrenewable resources. Mechanical engineers are now looking for ways to reduce their impact on the environment. Some are developing machines and processes that

> **Fossil fuels** are sources of energy that are formed within Earth from plants or animals. These are coal, oil, or natural gas.

> Coal-burning plants, like this one, are useful, but they can cause a lot of air pollution.

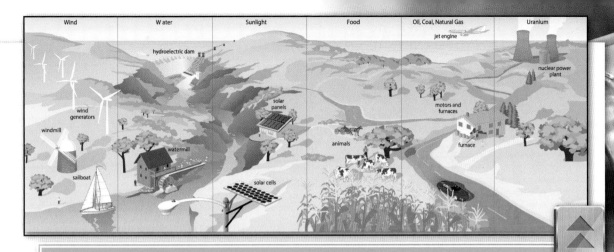

This diagram shows several energy sources in nature that people use for food and power.

produce fewer pollutants and use renewable power sources, such as water, sunlight, wind, and heat from within Earth. All can be used to make electricity.

Hydroelectric dams use the energy of moving water to make electricity. Solar cells convert sunlight into electricity, and wind turbines use wind energy to make electrical or mechanical energy. Hot water or steam from below ground—geothermal energy—can also be used to make electricity. Mechanical engineers are working to build upon these advances and apply them to existing machines and systems.

The Human Machine

The human body is the most complicated machine. Bioengineering is a mechanical engineering specialty. Many bioengineers focus on creating and improving prosthetic devices. Prosthetic devices are used to help or replace natural functions of the body. They include artificial hands, limbs, eyes, ears, and teeth. They also include hearing aids and pacemakers. Not only do prosthetic devices have to work well, they must be comfortable, too.

There are also prosthetic replacements for some organs and tissues. The heart-lung machine, which consists

Prosthetic devices such as this leg help improve people's lives.

of an artificial lung and a pump, is used during open-heart surgery. A mechanical heart-assist device can act as a real heart for a time. Blood vessels can be replaced with tiny tubes. A dialysis machine can clean blood and add important substances to it. Other artificial body parts under development include replacements for bones.

THINK ABOUT IT

Besides mechanical engineering, what other kinds of study would a bioengineer need to focus on to develop useful products for people's bodies?

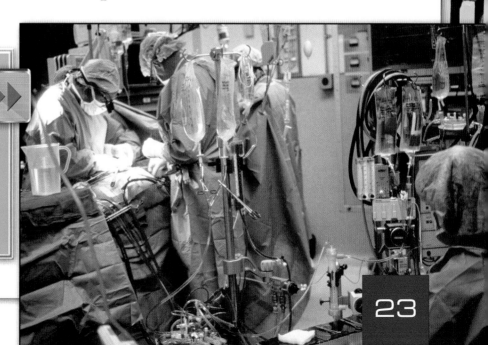

A heart-lung machine takes over the functions of the heart and lungs during surgery.

ROBOTICS

Robotics is another specialty of mechanical engineering. Robots can be programmed to perform tasks, and some can change what they do depending on their "senses." Robots are not necessarily in human form. A robot might just be an arm-like machine with motors.

Robots are often used in factories to assemble parts and products. Robots can do the same task over and over at different speeds. They are also used in many situations that could be dangerous to people, such as disabling bombs, performing tasks in outer space, and exploring areas of the ocean where humans cannot go.

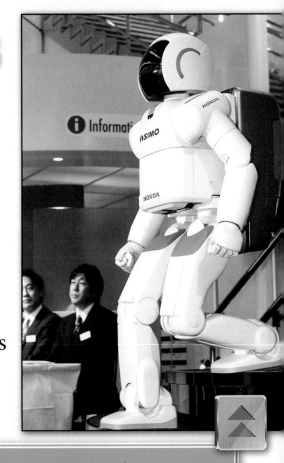

The robot Asimo shows how it can walk down stairs. Most robots cannot move like humans.

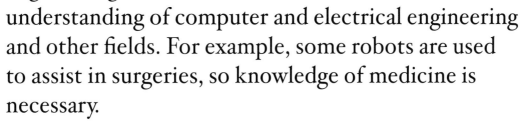

Robotic arms such as these can make accurate cuts and perform other actions during surgery.

Robotics engineers combine knowledge of mechanical engineering with an understanding of computer and electrical engineering and other fields. For example, some robots are used to assist in surgeries, so knowledge of medicine is necessary.

COMPARE AND CONTRAST

A robotic arm might be needed in undersea and space exploration. How would the different conditions in each of these settings present challenges for an engineer?

How to Become a Mechanical Engineer

All successful mechanical engineers have certain qualities. They are creative and are good problem solvers. They must be excellent communicators and work well with others. If you are interested in a career as a mechanical engineer, you can practice these qualities. You can also study hard in math and science in school.

Mechanical engineers attend college for 4 or 5 years. Many mechanical engineering programs also provide hands-on experience, which means you can work on different kinds of projects yourself. In the United States,

Engineers—young and old—never stop asking questions about how things work.

If they choose to become mechanical engineers, students may work on a life-size wind turbine some day.

engineers must take a test to begin working. The test is called the Fundamentals of Engineering exam. Those who pass are called engineers in training or engineer interns. Then, they work for about 4 years. Finally, they take the Principles and Practice of Engineering exam to receive a full license as an engineer.

Think About It

Even after attending school and taking two exams, engineers in many states are required to take classes. How do you think continuing their education keeps engineers at their best? What would happen if they did not continue learning?

ENGINEERING IN ACTION

Windmills use wind to power machines. Try making your own!

Materials: an empty juice carton, a pen, a ruler, a thin wooden rod, a small paper cup, string, a Styrofoam ball about 3 inches (7.5 centimeters) wide, index cards, tape, and popsicle sticks

Mechanical engineers can create machines that use wind and the sun to power our world.

1. Use the ruler and pen to make a hole about 1.75 inches (4.5 centimeters) below the flat part of the carton, centered horizontally.
2. Repeat on the opposite side of the carton.
3. Put the rod through the two holes.

4. Attach a paper cup to the string. Tie the other end to the rod.
5. Push the Styrofoam ball onto the other side of the rod.
6. Cut four equal-sized pieces of index cards and tape each to a popsicle stick to make the windmill blades. Place them in the Styrofoam ball at an angle.
7. Put your windmill in front of a blowing fan. If the blades are in the right place, they will turn the rod and raise the cup.

That is wind power! How could a machine like this be used in real life?

Your windmill may look something like this. Get creative, and make it colorful!

GLOSSARY

artificial Not natural. Made, produced, or done to seem like something natural.

boiler A large container in which water is heated to produce steam in an engine.

convert To change something into a different form so that it can be used in a different way.

design To plan and make something for a specific use or purpose.

develop To create something over a period of time or to make something better or more advanced.

generator A machine by which mechanical energy is changed into electrical energy.

gravity The force that causes things to fall toward Earth.

horizontally Positioned from side to side rather than up and down.

hydroelectricity Electricity produced by machines that are powered by moving water.

license An official document that gives permission to do, use, or have something.

motor A rotating machine that transforms electrical energy into mechanical energy.

nonrenewable Unable to be continually replaced by nature.

perishable Likely to spoil or decay quickly.

programmed Having a set of instructions to perform a particular action.

research To study to find or report new knowledge about something.

specialized Made or used for one particular purpose, job, or place.

structure Something that is built by putting parts together and that usually stands on its own.

turbine An engine that has a part with blades that are caused to spin by pressure from water, steam, or air.

For More Information

Books

Biskup, Agnieszka, and Tammy Enz. *Super Cool Science and Engineering Activities with Max Axiom, Super Scientist.* North Mankato, MN: Capstone Press, 2015.

Enz, Tammy. *Zoom It: Invent New Machines That Move.* Mankato, MN: Capstone Press, 2012.

Hagler, Gina. *Top STEM Careers in Engineering.* New York, NY: Rosen Publishing, 2015.

Herweck, Don. *Mechanical Engineering.* Mankato, MN: Compass Point Books, 2009.

Snedden, Robert. *Mechanical Engineering and Simple Machines.* St. Catharines, ON: Crabtree Publishing Company, 2013.

Websites

Because of the changing nature of Internet links, Rosen Publishing has developed an online list of websites related to the subject of this book. This site is updated regularly. Please use this link to access the list:

http://www.rosenlinks.com/LFO/Mech

Index